Pakistan the Land of Corruption, Mafias, Militias, Gangs

Background & Introduction:

People will think about it that I am giving the wrong face, wrong picture, Bad Picture of Pakistan (The Whole Nation), In this I am using hate speech or allegedly saying something about someone, twisting facts, using twisting words to alter realties/ground realities

Past Writings Against Pakistan:
(Speaking about Whole Nation)

In Past when someone written anything positive or negative about Pakistan, the motives of them people were to hit Pakistan, and the image of whole Nation or somewhat similar to that Painting the whole nation with one Brush, According to the ideology/mentality of the writer.

Credibility, Social Status of Writer Being a Expert:

In my case I am not a expert, political expert, My opinion is just opinion as lay man, A lay man who don't assume too much things on his own, who don't develop the perception about society, people, system and other matters from micro to macro level on his own assumptions.

Criteria to Verify & Merits to speak Against Nation as whole:
(The Blind Intellects, Educated through forefathers n Women in Pakistan)

What is the case or criteria to verify anything, when you are speaking about a Nation and Massive Corruption's Wholes, which are not filled due to Over Greed of Intellects of Pakistan, the blind intellects of Pakistan, which are permanently blind due to over-hunger, over thirst, over greed of corruption by their parents, by their women in society, from lower to lower middle to upper class, everyone are same in hunger, greed, thirst to do corruption in Pakistan.

<u>100-150 Families, Grabbing Pakistani Nation as Mafias, Militias, Gangs:</u>

When you speak about Pakistani Politics, You can name few leaders in Pakistan and Pakistani Intellect, Average Muslim, Average Human being is always through media, political experts, opinion makers in Pakistan, they always force you to idealize them as Genuine, Ideal Leader

Infect No Leader of Pakistan, since 1947 was sincere with Pakistan, 100% dedicated, spent his life who ever thought about Pakistan, who Practically Day and Night Spent to Build this Nation Practically a Ideal Muslim Nation like Far-East or Western Democratic Example State

1)Obeying Allah and His Messenger's Life

2) Made any Islamic code Politio, Socio, Economically

3)Drafted any laws which are compatible with Modern world in Pakistan

4)Drafted any laws, which will made Institutions in Pakistan

5)Drafted any laws, which will genuinely make any genuine, Islamic or Western Courts which will do speedy Justice

6)Drafted any laws, which will guide people friendly, help them in their life to obtain solutions for their matters in society

7) Drafted any policies in which Finance, Credit, Loans Non Interest (Islamic Principles of Sood/Interest/Markup/LAIBOR

or Ribah/Usuary Free) or Western any law of Credit like leasing for every item, for every person on Federal, Provincial Government

INSTITUTE

8)Who made any practical ways to build Institutions, State/Centralized Bank Policies, which will favor the lay man, for every basic necessity would be responsibility of the state as per Western Democratic or Islamic Law

9) Who made any Education Institutions, who will taught the Education Technical & Religious Islamic education from Primary to Secondary to Higher, Graduation, Masters Level who will produce Intellect Muslims, who will contribute in the

society as Intellect Muslim, in Jobs, Business, Departments of the Society on Regional, Provincial, National, International Level

10) Who developed the thoughts, guidance, about that who is Leader? What is Political Leadership? And why this is necessary in this time period to become a Political Leader, who will bring Investments, Finance, Management, Administration, and Finance through local sources, resources of state, or from foreign outside Project Finance Companies, from or through Foreign Collateral Services Providers who will establish Credit Limits and Finance for Nation

International Finance

100-150 Families, Using Pakistan as Sex-Slave, Debating that rights of this Pakistan should be Islamic sex-slave rights or western sex slave rights:

In Pakistan, All of the families since the time Muhammad Ali Jinnah (Bani-e-Pakistan) formed the Pakistan, based on Two Nation Theory that (Hindu & Muslims) are not able to tolerate them, in terms of culture, religions, and they cannot live under same roof, constitution, law

When Liaqat Ali Khan became the first president of Pakistan and Quaide Azam became the Governor General of East and West Pakistan, Consisted of two wings, and In 1947 Indo-Pakistan Kashmir Region Fight started

The house passed it on 12 March 1949. It has been described as the "Magna Carta" of Pakistan's constitutional history. Both United States and Soviet Union sent invitation to Liaqat Ali Khan. However, Khan chose to first pay a goodwill visit to United States. This was perceived as a rebuff to Moscow, and has been traced to profound adverse consequences. Khan had wanted Pakistan to remain neutral in the Cold War, as declared three days after Pakistan's independence when he declared that Pakistan would take no sides in the conflict of ideologies between the nations. Khan later tried to visit Soviet Union but the dates for goodwill visit were not materialized by Soviet Union.

12 March, 1949, Magna Carta, of Pakistan Constitutional History, Under uni-nateral agreement of Soviet Union and United States described and Mr Liaqat Ali Khan Pay a good will visit to United states, in this time period Urdu has been declared as official Lanaguage of Pakistan,

However there was a protest in East Pakistan or East Bengal that Bengali is the language and most people speak benagli language and in this controversy Jinnah also faced problems, when Douglas Gracey refused to obey orders of Mr Jinnah,

And in argument He said that Jinnah as Governor General represented the British Crown and as appointee he is acting person, therefore refused and didn't sent the troops to Kashmir.

The standing orders of Mr. Jinnah was refused by Air Vice Marshal Richard Atcherley and Commander in chief of Navy Rear Admiral James Wifred Jefford who also refused the standing orders of Mr Jinnah, In the time period of Liaqat Ali Khan India & Pakistan decided to solve this issue of Kashmir peacefully, However and 1st January, 1949 it was decided as Free Plebiscite State under the supervision of UN.

ANTI ARMY AND PRO ARMED FORCES:

The Rule of Power & Performances:

Pakistani Leaders, Armed Forces, Civilian Mentality About Wealth:

1. History is witness, when there is difference of opinion, then creating it a dispute/fight/war b/w two parties/groups people/factors those mafias, militias, who can get benefit from the fight/dispute b/w two groups, they always use every type of theoretical, ideological, political, religious literature in order to create flames and fire so they can achieve their burning targets, In 1956,

1)people are produced in programs, media houses, article writers in news paper, who praise/criticize 2 Head of states of Pakistan, 1 is General Ziaul Haq, 2nd is Zulfiqar Ali Bhutto, and they conclude as,

2.Bhutto/Zia was great "democratic/islamic" leaders, they have done this, they have done this, 1 made the democracy, law, constitution mafia based constitution drafting, broken Pakistan, his sons also ran campaign against Pakistan Army Al Zulfiqar, and other terrorist organizations they were working against Pakistan Army and Pakistan

3. Zulfiqar Ali Bhutto broken & destroyed Pakistan and made East Pakistan in partying the Mujeeb ur Rehman in Pakistan, in 1971, Due to Nixson and Cossegen Pakistan was saved by chance, otherwise in 7-8 days, it would have been vanished or it will be a part of Great India again, but this is not done, but it has given the power and privilege to 100-150 families, and who remained keep on using it as sex slave till today the whole nation is paralyzed due to them

The difference of opinion was used

"Tame surrender to Indians on Issue of Kashmir" on the name of Peaceful Solution in Supervision of UN or It is Actually Political Solution which will be solved through International law and Solution

United Nations

OVERDOSED, DIZZLING FAINTED/NEAR TO DEATH UNO:

In present time period, Till today, UN (United Nations) is intoxicated by High and Over Dose Drug of Morphine, Cocaine, Alcohol, In the Hibernation period, Feeling in state of Dream/Faintness, Near to death, in which cardiac rhythm and slow respiration UNO is getting and though they are marked as Alive/Breathing,

But Till today, 2016, April With the Blessings of International Democratic Champions, Leaders, War Leaders, International Joint Venture participants of War Leaders "Kashmir", is not declared as separate independent state like referendum of Ireland or many other examples in History you can give, But Kashmir would not become a Separate state

Due to Ego of Bharat Desh or Jiey Hind or India the Great Nation, Which can shed blood of 100's and 1000's of the people per day, Mujahideen/Fighters/Freedom Fighters, Gangs, Trans-Nation Crime Indo-Pak, Military Border line crimes or what ever

But we will not say yes to that, due to it is matter of our ego and prestige, India the Land of Cheap Mentality & Superiority Complex Or Hind Superiority Complex

Gangs working in Pakistan Right now:

Structure & Formation of Gangs:

The gangs have rule, once if you are not caught, then who the hell can call you criminal first

Second if you are caught, then yet we have choice of media, we will pay to media, Media Houses we have made 100 channels, and media is blackmailing hot business in Pakistan, if you have done rape, if you have corruption, pay us money or otherwise evidence/proof we will expose you Internationally on satellite channel,

You will be exposed and portrayed as "criminal" or "personality primary culprit involve in crime" may be case you have a slight doubt/background, but it will take you 100 years to go to court of law and prove it, But in media how we will portray you, you and your family would not be able to walk in society as innocent or you have done nothing

If you are caught, media also behaved neutral and evidence against you are too much less, then we have ways for you

1. Litigations in court of law, due to you know that in this country 99% people says Islamic, Islamic, Islamic, but everything in Pakistan, when it comes to political/state matter, it is pure British

2. What is British, due to India was British colony and Some India, Some British Acts, and PPC AND CRPC (Pakistan Penal Code & Criminal Procedure Code)

3. In Journalist, writers or if anyone will dare to write anything against court of law or systems of lower, majistrate, banking, anti corruption, labors courts then issue them showcause notice, if not appeared then arrest warrant or non bailable warrants will be issued and no one inshallah/God willingly in this country will be able to think about speaking about system how judiciary works

Show Cause Notice.

- A Show Cause Notice is an official document
- inviting you to show cause or justify to Council
- why Council should not issue you with an
- Enforcement Notice to remedy the alleged
- breach of legislation. If you do not attend the
- hearing or respond in one of the other ways
- indicated in the Notice, Council will issue an
- Enforcement Notice.
- Failure to comply with an
- Enforcement Notice is of itself an offence.

4. How judiciary works it have Before Partition Indian system like "Paishkaars" in adalat/courts, manual files, manual files thrown out in shelves, 1000kg= metric tons, 20-50-100 mton is weight of files, papers on which suit, writ, petitions are filed that will be on paper and will remain on paper and in that 2 security guards who are

taking weapons of nawabs carrying in hand for security this is court in Pakistan

IMAGE OF CITY COURT KARACHI, IN WHICH 100'S OF COURTS ARE WORKING IN PATTERN OF SIKANDARE AZAM, 100% SYSTEM IS ADOPTED FROM THE IDEA OF STONE AGE AND WHAT IS ADDED, TYPE WRITERS, COMPUTERS, MILLIONS AND BILLIONS TONS OF PAPERS, UPON PAPERS, AND 1 PETITION, COURT, BALIF, COURT, NOTICE, HEARING YOU WILL GET IN 120 YEARS MINIMUM (INSHALLAH/GOD WILLING)

IMAGE 2 OF CITY/LOWER COURT KARACHI PAKISTAN

IMAGE 3 OF CITY COURT KARACHI PAKISTAN

5. Paying 100-200-500-1000 rupees PKR in documentation, type writer, suit, petition filing process based all filed and all record registrars is necessary, no staff of any court/government will submit or take even infect any file in Pakistan

6. In lower courts Alhamdulillah/God's Grace 100-200-500-1000 rupees paying is compulsory, if you will come to the court of law, the Nation who was made on the name of Islam "Speaking about Justice for world, on the name of Islam" "The nation and their ideological and Islamic speakers claim that Islam give solution for humanity, they don't have solution for themselves

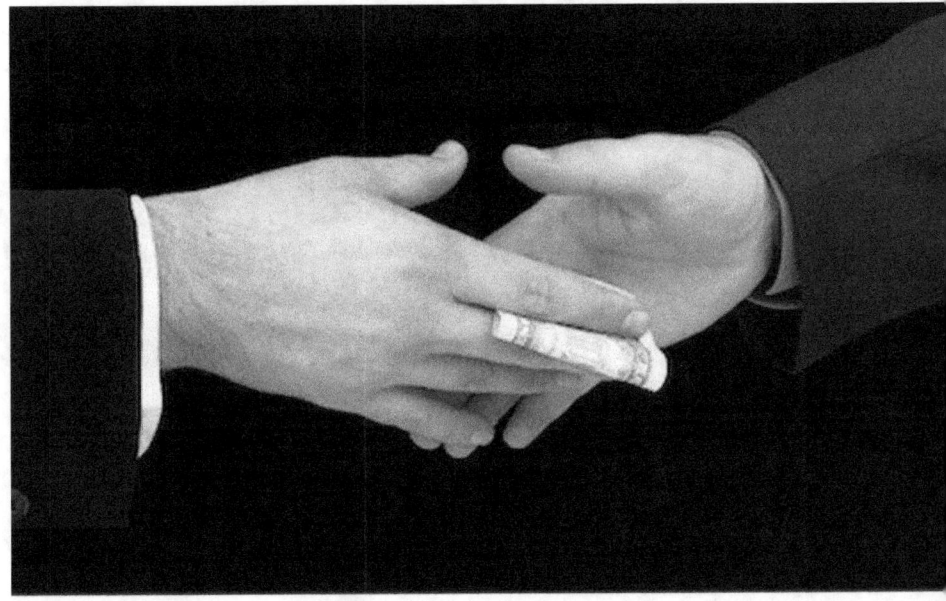

7. The Nation which speaks about Islamic Sovereignty, that God is Hakim, Hakmiat is for Allah Tabarakwatalla/God Almighty, it means the extra ordinary litigated system, which can destroy the life of individuals, childs, females, males, once you are arrested, you are innocent or guilty,

Inshallah/God Willingly by mistake/fluke if your file comes then you are more than lucky, it is infect you are more lucky then the one person in movies, who is sent to ring of death to fight and you don't know the basic fighting and Person with swords and armors ready to fight & kill you

8. There are courts categorized like Domain wise, like labor, anti-corruption, banking courts, in which judiciary is divided in sub-category, in Islam 99% courts work as general courts, if issue of banking/financial or dispute, there would be no law made especially for banks, financial laws, taxation laws, social, family, criminal laws, complications upon complications, acts and acts reformations upon reformations not only destroys the justice infect it never ever will give justice to anyone this is moral teachings of Islam

9. Why Banking/Financial/Labor laws and violation of laws, and crime/offense is done, in banking/financial matters, social/family/criminal matters there are 90% cases which a lay man justice can do, by analyzing who need justice and who is offended

In Civil/Family/Criminal Jurisdiction
we don't need ministry of law, we need a department who will draft violation of basic commandments, it will make you criminal according to stage

For example

1.If husband or wife had a fight, and they hitted each other in fight or male is strong physically, if there is any physical more damage, then fine/penalty/financial penalty immediately on sight in the court of law it would be done (so in order to save females from violations of basic human rights laws, no one should exercise power in order to offend anyone)

if due to anger/frustration or anything is not major complex, then counselors females and males which would be Muslim/part of court of law, will guide them, in frustration or tension or depression, make a good life and make a good living and don't fight each other, if fighting reason for them is "financial stability" due to it is Islamic compulsory law, that for every needs of a individual female/male it is responsibility of state to complete that state

if female need husband or male need husband at age of 12/13/14 or when you reach puberty age, and marriage at this stage and entering in a relationship and finding financial solution, family arrangement, education basic matriculation/intermediate/high school, how and who will earn the money, and what are responsibilities and to guide them, to finance them

(According to Islam, According to Guidance of Rasoolullah saw and Allah it is compulsory for state to fulfill that basic needs otherwise state is not "khalifah/representative of God on the face of the Earth, which can make a system of "Justice & Equality" based system,

From Administrator to peon or CEO of company (salary, money earnings should be offered, must be offered by employers, Government/Private, should/must be based on Social Justice & Equality

Injustice In Pakistan

10. But in Pakistan, Injustice flows in the veins of Pakistan, the civilians who is poor is worst then animals on streets, and infect 6-7-10 people die every day on Highway, same dies in USA I know, and No one reports that in USA & Pakistan also, but they have many many things, which we will not have in 168 Next Years Due to this is the state made on the name of Islam

Allah (swt)

11. Hakmiat/Sovereignty in Pakistan is for Allah tala/God Almighty, But Ruling Party are Gangs always, 6-7 Gangs and 100-150 Families, Feudals, Law Enforcement Establishment Mafia (who make/bring corrupt and most corrupt people as infect no one should employ them on a scale of labor/peon also, what the hell they knows about federation/state/province/law at all

12. In Banking/Criminal Laws in Islam & Pakistan Pakistan should make laws like pattern of Israel there is not such special codes and format of rules

Rights protected by Basic Law: Human Dignity and Liberty

The rights protected by this law are detailed in several clauses:[4]

- Section 1: The purpose of this Basic Law is to protect human dignity and liberty, in order to establish in a Basic Law tile values of the State of Israel as a Jewish and democratic state.
- Section 2: There shall be no violation of the life, body or dignity of any person as such.
- Section 3: There shall be no violation of the property of a person.
- Section 4: All persons are entitled to protection of their life, body and dignity.
- Section 5: There shall be no deprivation or restriction of the liberty of a person by imprisonment, arrest, extradition or otherwise.
- Section 6:
  - (a) All persons are free to leave Israel.
  - (b) Every Israeli national has the right of entry into Israel from abroad.
- Section 7:
  - (a) All persons have the right to privacy and to intimacy.
  - (b) There shall be no entry into the private premises of a person who has not consented thereto.
  - (c) No search shall be conducted on the private premises of a person, nor in the body or personal effects.
  - (d) There shall be no violation of the confidentiality of conversation, or of the writings or records of a person.

However, several cardinal human rights are missing from this document, such as the Right for Equality, Freedom of Speech, Freedom of Religion, Freedom of Protest, and others. These rights were given to the residents of Israel by general principles which existed before this Basic Law. Although these rights were not included in the law, some jurists, such as former President of The Supreme Court of Israel Aharon Barak, see these rights are directly derived from the "right to dignity".

so such type of common laws, for marriage, divorce, you can make
Banks for personal, business and international banking and transactions as per laws and regulations of international regulations have to take opinion in

Credit, Borrowing, Interest, Usuary, Markup based

leasing/purchase lending in stock/brokerage houses, securities, investment companies

should and must not invest in tobacco, heroine, morphene, cocaine, drugs in general, alcohol, pornography, digital/manual marketing companies who are marketing porn industry, investment in projects of such activities they are doing

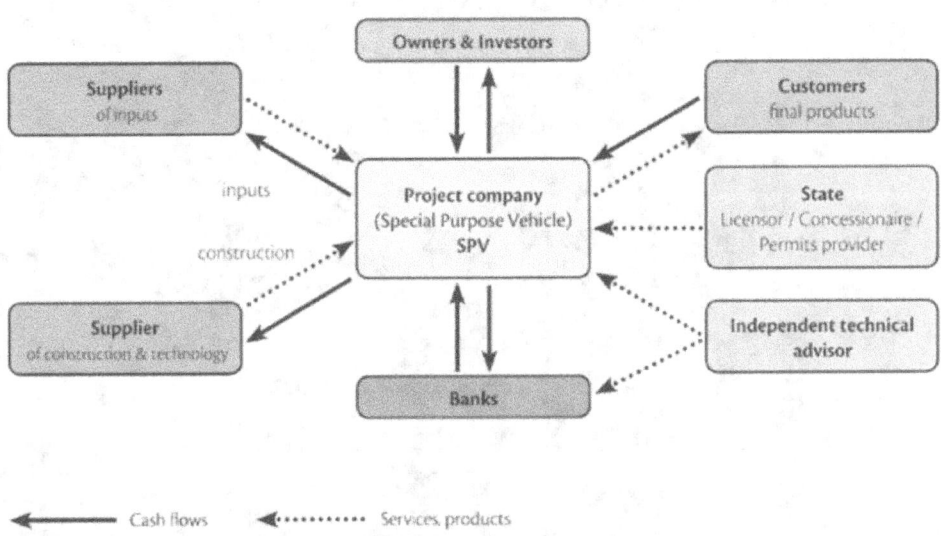

Notes:
Sponsors may be beside an investor also in a role of a supplier, a customer or the state – accordingly how much the subject is incerested on a particular project and what risks it bears. Some roles may overlap (e.g. investor and customer).

otherwise borrowing from International states, Joint venture, trade, project, trade project finance, for oil refinery, hospital, health structure, power, infra-structure, oil refineries, power projects on nation/state level (You can do, But everything is possible, may be Pakistan can become More progressive than UAE/OMAN/BEHRAIN) but how Industries, Agriculture, Science, Technology, Basic Primary Education to Secondary Education to PhD nothing we will do and Inshallah/God willingly in 168 years, we will be rotting in this hell due to this hell was burnt by 100-150 families, they are fix by God as destiny over us, they are born to rule us, we are born to be ruled by them

Project Mafia:

if you are in Pakistan and you can get project finance for developing

1.Train Railway From Pakistan to India to other countries, Afghanistan, Iran, Russian Track of CIS countries Speed Rail

2.if you are able to bring project finance in the form of project financing bank guarantees or finance cash project financing against bank guarantees then bring it, 5billion is worth of project, pay us 20% then you will be allowed to operate in Pakistan (For Development of Pakistan,

For Development of Primary Education, Primary Woman Development, Basic Human Rights, Jails Grave Yards Humanitarian Projects, Commercialize projects in which private entity and state will earn money

3.Project is going to be done/completed in Pakistan or not, this is not matter, the matter is give us 5-10-20-30% money in that then how we are going to earn the money?

Sasti Roti, Laptop Distribution Project, Yellow Cab, Vehicles Routing Project in Pakistan like Suzuki/mini truck for loading, metro and orange line train in project of 5billion 20billion$ 30% kickback commission and 80% corruption from that Alhamdulillah these gangs are alive and 100-150 families they are since childhood I am listening the name of them

WHY TALIBAN DON'T BLAST NATIONAL, PROVINCIAL ASSEMBLIES, SUPREME, HIGHER, LOWER COURTS:

Talibans are made in USA, Trained by CIA, then Osama Bin laden is the picture or media target of illuminatis or freemasonaries or what, But He came to Arab Countries, Black Gold oil, Financial & Religious supports references for him made, later on independence or writ of Islamic Government came in Afghanistan Russian Conflict

Pakistan participated, Arab Countries, G20, USA, UK, EU Countries supported, at that time Talibans were Good people, According to Benazir Bhutto She said and Robin Rofel she also said that

To a senior Journalist they have given presentation by FIA & Minister of Information that they are very good people and we have to do some work in Joint venture of them

Later on Taliban came in Pakistan, "Taliban" is Label, Any Criminal has to keep beard, ware kameez+shalwaar, and hold the turban and purchase weapon, due to Government specially Sindh Government in Pakistan issued 100,000's of license to make money inside that domain also,

Sindh Government and Asif Ali Zardari+Faryal Talpure, Muzaffar Tapi+Syed Qaim Ali shah, they imported Terrorist from Tanzania, killed 5000 people in liyari and many areas of Karachi.

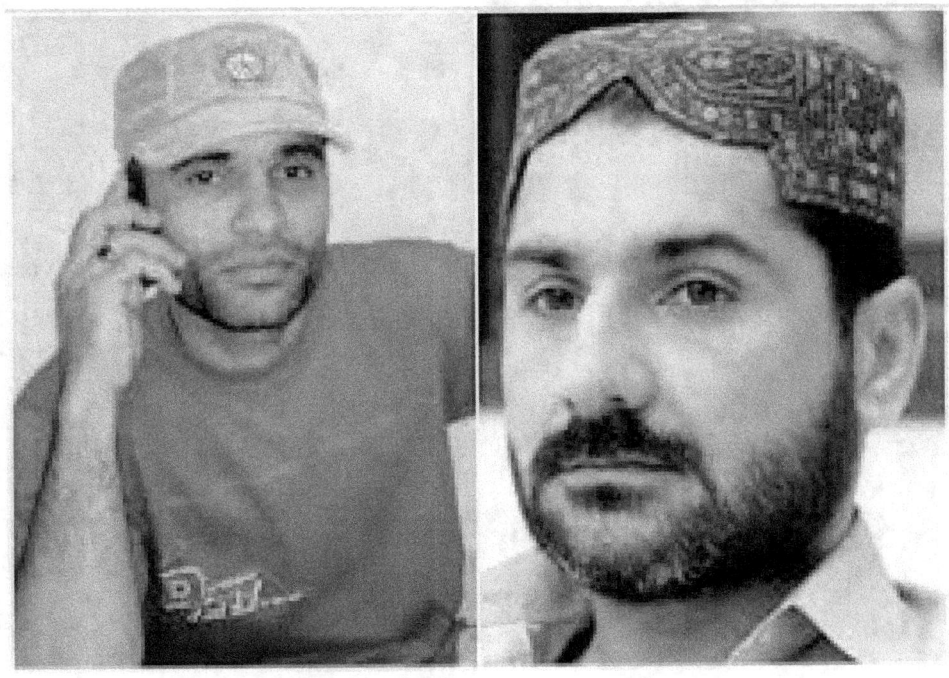

In every Sindh government 80-90% criminals are working/employed in Karachi, some are appointed by haqiqi, some are appointed by mqm, pppp, and every party and funds and Recently Supreme court of Pakistan chief Justice said that

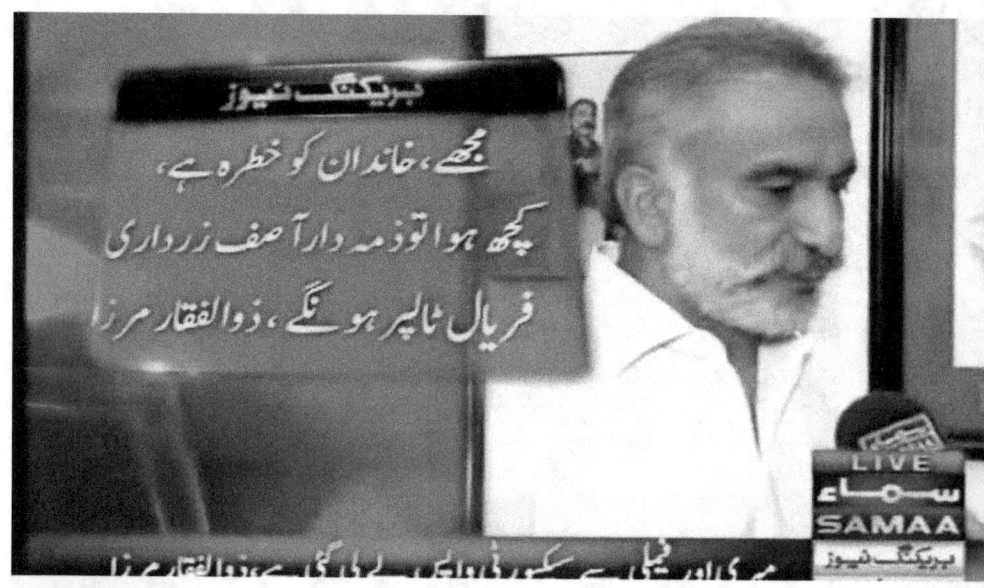

1. In crore of the rupees thanas/police stations are sold and those who paid that much amount money, they are recovering+multiplying it

2.In any court of the law if you will speak that "this mr +honorable judges are corrupt In Pakistan, you will get the "show cause notice" you will be arrested for 10-20-30-50 years, Inshallah/God willingly if you don't have money or property or any bail to defend you, how you alleged to a honorable court of law's on service judge?

In Islamic countries, Judges are servant to states, 24 hours/365/7 days, Head of state are servant for state, state has to respect them, and their order will be implemented, but judges and their protocols are not lesser then British Lords? Then what is problem in British or American Style of Society, why this drama of Islamic countries, Islamic law we have since 68 years, why we need Islam for what? For this British Lords Based Courts we need Islamic courts or what?

Or we are waiting for more gangs/groups to be made by Hilary Clinton to shed some blood or dirt on the name of "Islam/Jihad" ??!!!

3.In Panama Leaks the on duty Judge, His Name & Judges and Cartoons came & appear on social media but on television news channels the name of that judge not came, due to media is already paid, in Pakistan every column writer daily praise a specific persons, related to any group like someone supporting jamate islami, some praising mqm, some praising pppp, some praising others, how much groups/handful groups are there

They are praising like they are angel or divine personalities and they are last and first hope for them?

4.In Pakistan the country has no

1.Desalination plants for sea/river water, millions of fishes died every year, due to "mixing of severage water in sea water" that same water Alhamdulillah we are drinking by God's Grace

DESALINATION

- It is a process that removes or separates salts from saline water to give fresh water, at the expense of energy.
- Depending upon the type or form of energy used, Desalination Processes can be broadly classified into two groups:
1. Thermal Desalination
2. Membrane Desalination

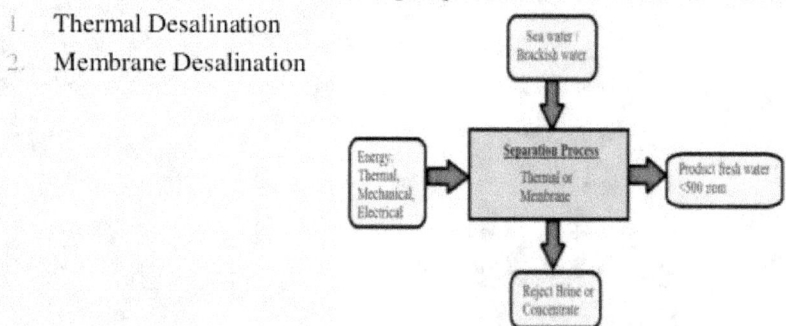

In Pakistan small fishes are caught and eggs of fishes are caught in net

due to in breeding or season of breeding time period, 50% of the banned time period, Handful people who are able to pay the money for whole season, the money is paid and launches, net are allowed secretly and Everything is getting destroyed and we have no comparison in fish, or fish industry as compare to India but we are destroying it more

In Pakistan

sea ramp and 1 tv host was interviewing what government is doing there in gawadar the land and development cost for that and office for gawadar development government based in Karachi they found however, the civilians & resident will get nothing

IMAGE OF CURRENT LAUNCHES WE ARE USING IN
PAKISTAN

(TO WHAT LEVEL WE SHOULD/MUST BE UPGRADED, DUE TO CURRENT STATUS
UPDATING WE NEVER THOUGHT SINCE 30 LAST YEARS AT ALL)

In Pakistan how Afghanis are illegal refuges or don't have
CNIC OF PAKISTAN, they are in Pakistan same as iranis are
baloch are through Baluchistan and Iran are here in Pakistan,

and 200 years back wood launches, and new motor launches, China is manufacturing and Korea/Japan with auto net and graph and indicators required for depth of water, fishing required, we don't have to do nothing in that

2.In UAE, 1 party informed me a Mineral water sufficient for a beaurucrate family for 3 months, consignment going to Karachi due to they don't drink the water of Pakistan also, due to it is well known fact all of the leaders

1.Their sons, Like Imran khan's sons are getting educated in UK, He is in consent with his wife, making and raising them in UK, due to his son's life will be destroyed in Pakistan, and sometime they came in Pakistan for his election campaign

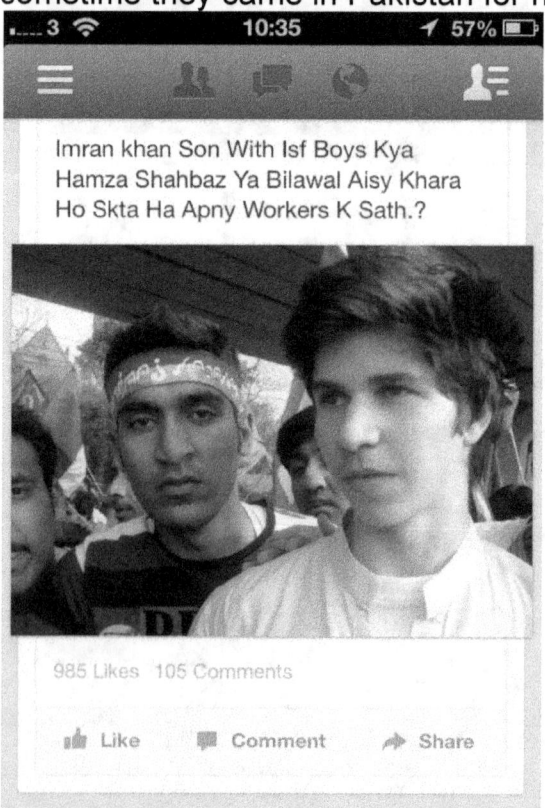

people are happy, that 1 leader/fake revolutionist, A Single unmarried Single Man, is living in 7000sq yard, home, I as Male with 4 wives and 10 sons having 400-600-800-1000sq yard homes, all of the 4 in the life time, I don't need any major alteration in it, sufficient for me, my future 1 more generation or more due to you don't need that much space to live with comfort, but people are happy, some leader imported/invited for few days, then they departed, they are happy that stood with some workers of party (that's our level of acceptance, and our level of mentality, what we consider us)

2.Nawaz Shareef, Zardari, Bilawal they are not in Pakistan, Aseefa, Bakhtawar all of them are in UAE, ZURICH 12 months, they came here to rule Pakistan, due to 12 months they are not in Pakistan, in Dubai/Zurich they are

Equivalent to Billions of PKR Property with name of Bilawal House and other properties in 70 Clifton they made in Lahore BEHRIA TOWN AND KARACHI PAKISTAN

52% people don't have food to eat 2 times, a son of ex-prime minister in Pakistan living like kings in Pakistan, 99% time He spent in UAE, comes in Pakistan with 200 guards, local police, Sindh government's special protocol and paid people 500-1000rs to come in Jalsa, he deliver speech, do the tweets, on the name of Bhutto & ziaulhaq, his father who murdered his wife/mother of bilawal their son and daughters knows that also, that Asif Ali Zardari Murdered Meer Murtaza Bhutto & Benazir Both (still campaigning and using this place as place to visit annually or 2 3 times/year basis)

3.Asif Ali Zardari, Faryal Talpure Murdered Benazir, After Benazir +Zardari successfully murdered Meer Murtaza Bhutto and Asif Ali Zardari+Faryal Talpure imported terrorist from Baluchistan, Iran, Tanzania also,

میں نے اپنی آنکھوں سے آغا فخر کو فریال تالپور کے بیڈروم میں جاتے دیکھا
ذوالفقار مرزا نے لائیو شو میں زرداری کی بہن کو بدچلن اور بدکردار قرار دے دیا

APP131-21
LARKANA: June 21 – President Asif Ali Zardari exchanging views with MNA Ms. Faryal Talpur during a public gathering in connection with 56th birth anniversary of Shaheed Mohtarma Benazir Bhutto at Naudaro House. APP photo by Jahangir Khan

عزیز بلوچ نے بے نظیر قتل کے گواہوں کو قتل کرنے، منی لانڈرنگ اور دیگر جرائم کا اعتراف کر لیا،

They beheaded 5000 civilians and threat of death and parchi/bhatta they collected from Karachi and Alhamdulillah yet they are contesting in elections, According to Uzair Baloch He said He has given map to Iran for Nuclear Plant of Pakistan and imported terrorist from Tanzania and Via Sea Route smuggled Launches/Boats to UAE, it is deposited in UAE BANKS, PROPERTIES ARE PURCHASED against it

In what category, on what's name and whose name the properties, account of money laundering is done, everything He informed to police and law enforcement agencies but no arrest or detention warrant and cases against bilawal, faryal talpure and zardari is issued, due to FIA, CIA, PAKISTANI FEDERAL GOVT is paid billions of amount or political black mailing to Shareef Family Government that

صولت مرزا کے بعد عزیر بلوچ نے بھی سنسنی خیز انکشافات کی ویڈیو ریکارڈ کرا دی

Listen we are coming in power after you, and we can ditch your government, so using both tactics Inshallah in 168 Years no Genuine leader in Pakistan will come due to we are born as slave and they are born to rule us as Leaders/Kings

In Pakistan gangs using name of Taliban & Tehreke Taliban Pakistan they are Indian, Iranian Agents, terrorists, foreign terrorists, they don't have any link to khilafat/islam, they have link

With the local government and establishment & law enforcement agencies, who are using criminals, killing them in killings raids of police and rangers once in blue moon or arrested or detained and using them in Jail also

JAIL POLICE:

The Jail police domain is different in Pakistan, every criminal & target killers, we are inspired by westerners, they are making programs of Jail Abroad on National Geographic Channel, But Every target killer of every party MQM, ANP, SUNNI TEHREEK, Sipahe Sahaba, Tehreeke Jafria, they are financed and their goods came in 8-10 hilux vehicles, 4 servant, in AAA+ Class Jail they are living

In Jails some of the times A Killer & Target killer is moved from the Jails and He goes out and murder 2-4 people, and came back, if you will ask (what is evidence) no evidence of any crime till the day of Judgment is possible in Pakistan,

Due to in court of law, Paishkaars, where CCTV Cameras are there, they came out of court room and take money, and in lower/higher to everywhere, in police, in every legal & law enforcement agencies how they operate corruption, and they bribe money from people, under boundaries and cover, in 120 years, you cannot say a word in front of 5 people and 10 people, leave the issue of speaking or corruption evidence is out of question?

Whoever is going to arrest, you will be bail out, if you are powerful and have money, no court will punish you 100000000000000% guaranteed in Pakistan always, and always and remain always same in 267 Years Next

KARACHI CCTV CAMERA:

In Pakistan cctv camera and other financing options never we indented to get project finance based on any bank/sovereign guarantee due to in Karachi, Lahore or anywhere we don't need any project finance, our city will never get, Punjab, Pakhtoonkhuah, Baluchistan, Sindh, Interior Sindh Never Ever we will get CCTV Cameras or monitoring and confirm monitoring of it and then action on it

In Police, those higher and senior persons are working/shotting/arresting/detaining people are employeed by political mafia and beaurucarcy and constitution mafia people and a civilian whose mother/father/brother is missing "in 120 years" police will not do any effort to search them in any manner, they will ask you 200 rupees to lodge fir or 2000 rupees, according to your capability and area where the thana is

جمعۃ المبارک 25 مارچ، 2011ء

روزنامہ امت کراچی

مُتحدہ دہشت گرد اجمل پہاڑی کے انکشافات پر کارروائی کی تیّاری

6 اعلیٰ پولیس افسران اسلام آباد طلب- 100 مقدمات میں نامزد اجمل مشرف دور میں پے رول پر رہا ہوا

کراچی (اسٹاف رپورٹر) دہشت گردی آپریشن میں سرگرم پولیس افسران و اہلکاروں اور سیاسی جماعتوں کے کارکنان کے قتل سمیت 100 سے زائد مقدمات میں مطلوب متحدہ قومی موومنٹ کے دہشت گرد شاہنواز عرف اجمل پہاڑی عرف عدنان کی سرکاری ذرائع نے تصدیق کر دی۔ ملزم مختلف عدالتوں سے سزا یافتہ اور مشرف حکومت میں پے رول پر رہا ہوا تھا۔ اسے نامعلوم مقام پر منتقل کر کے تفتیش کا دائرہ وسیع کر دیا گیا ہے۔ دوران تفتیش انکشافات کی بنیاد پر ایک فہرست مرتب کی گئی ہے اور پھر پور کارروائی کے لیے آئی بی ڈی، اسپیشل انوسٹی گیشن یونٹ اور انٹی وائلنٹ کرائم سیل کے 6 اعلیٰ افسران کو اسلام آباد طلب کر لیا گیا۔ ذرائع کے مطابق مسلسل ٹارگٹ کلنگ کے بعد حساس ادارے حرکت میں آئے اور 5 روز قبل سرجانی ٹاؤن سے اجمل پہاڑی کو گرفتار کر لیا گیا تاہم صدر آصف علی زرداری کے پارلیمنٹ کے مشترکہ اجلاس سے خطاب کے باعث اہم گرفتاری کو خفیہ رکھا گیا تھا تا کہ اتحادی جماعتوں کی سیاست کے باعث ملزم سے تفتیش متاثر نہ ہو سکے۔ ذرائع کے مطابق اجمل پہاڑی پر 1992 میں کراچی آپریشن میں سرگرم رہنے والے پولیس افسران و اہلکاروں، مخالف سیاسی جماعتوں کے رہنما و کارکنان اور 4 امریکی شہریوں سمیت قتل، اقدام قتل اور دہشت گردی کے 100 سے زائد مقدمات درج ہیں۔ ذرائع نے بتایا کہ وہ مشرف حکومت میں پے رول پر رہائی کے بعد روپوش ہوا تھا۔ ذرائع کے مطابق اجمل پہاڑی کے متحدہ سے وابستگی کے باعث گرفتاری کو صیغہ راز میں رکھا گیا ہے اور حساس اداروں کے اہلکار تمام تر تفتیش سے اسلام آباد کو آگاہ کر رہے ہیں، جس کی بنیاد پر پھر پور کارروائی کی تیاریاں مکمل کر لی گئی ہیں۔ اجمل پہاڑی کو 1998 میں 4 امریکیوں اور ان کے پاکستانی ڈرائیور کے قتل میں گرفتار کیا گیا تھا۔ 1997 میں پولیس مجھر ممتاز عرف مجھی کے قتل کا الزام بھی اس پر تھا۔ جب کہ پیپلز پارٹی کے کونسلر ظہیر اکرم ندیم اور مسلم لیگ (ن) اور جماعت اسلامی کے کارکنان کے قتل میں بھی ملوث رہا ہے۔ ذرائع کا کہنا ہے کہ اجمل پہاڑی سرجانی ٹاؤن سے اپنا نیٹ ورک چلا رہا تھا۔ اس کی ٹیم میں 16 سے زائد کارندے شامل ہیں جن میں نیو کراچی سیکٹر اور اورنگی ٹاؤن سیکٹر کے ٹارگٹ کلر شامل ہیں۔ اس حوالے سے گزشتہ دنوں امت نے تفصیلی رپورٹ شائع کی تھی، جس کے بعد حساس اداروں نے اس کے گرد گھیرا تنگ کرتے ہوئے اسے سرجانی ٹاؤن سے گرفتار کیا۔

☆☆☆☆☆

کراچی میں ٹارگٹ کلرز کو سیاسی پشت پناہی حاصل ہے

عسکری حکام

غیر ملکی ایجنسیوں کی سرگرمیاں حقیقت ہیں- 10 لاکھ سے زائد غیر قانونی طور پر مقیم ہیں- نکالا جائے- آئی ایس آئی کی بریفنگ

اسلام آباد (مانیٹرنگ ڈیسک/ایجنسیاں) سپریم کورٹ، رینجرز اور پولیس کے بعد ملک کے اہم ترین خفیہ ادارے آئی ایس آئی نے بھی کراچی میں قتل و غارت کی بڑی وجہ سیاسی پشت پناہی کو قرار دے دیا۔ کراچی میں خون خرابے اور قاتلوں کی سیاسی پشت پناہی کا نتیجہ کا سب سے پہلے سپریم کورٹ نے اپنے فیصلے میں لکھا، پھر ڈی جی رینجرز اور کراچی پولیس کے سربراہ نے سیاسی جماعتوں کو مورد الزام ٹھہرایا۔ اب آئی ایس آئی نے بھی کڑوا سچ عوامی نمائندوں کو بتا دیا ۔ ذرائع کے مطابق آئی ایس آئی حکام نے قومی اسمبلی کی قائمہ کمیٹی برائے دفاع کو بتایا کہ کراچی میں روز لاشیں گرنے کی ایک ہی بنیادی وجہ ہے کہ ٹارگٹ کلرز کو سیاسی پشت پناہی حاصل ہے۔ غیر ملکی ایجنسیوں کی پاکستان میں سرگرمیاں بھی حقیقت ہیں۔ قائمہ کمیٹی نے شہر قائد کی بگڑتی صورت حال پر ملک کی اہم ترین انٹیلی جنس ایجنسی کی بریفنگ کے بعد اتفاق کیا کہ کراچی آپریشن کی کامیابی کے لیے تمام سیاسی جماعتوں کو کردار ادا کرنا ہوگا۔ قبل ازیں سیکورٹی حکام نے اندرونی سلامتی پر بریفنگ دیتے ہوئے بتایا کہ کراچی میں 10 لاکھ سے زائد غیر ملکی شہری غیر قانونی طور پر مقیم ہیں، جو کہ دہشت گردی میں ملوث ہیں، جبکہ ملک بھر میں زیادہ تر افغان مہاجرین مجرمانہ سرگرمیوں میں ملوث پائے گئے۔ انہیں فوری طور پر ملک سے نکالنا چاہیے۔

☆ ☆ ☆ ☆ ☆

As Compare to India Police:

In India or secular countries there may be corruption more 5000% than Pakistan, but how much their police are working for either complains of harassment or lost or trafficking and how police are spending money and instead of teasing and torturing other citizens only some work or good work or at least some work they are doing, In Pakistan in next 180 years no one will work for civilians or any crime or criminal search

Due to who are criminal and police ask money and release them and fir if lodge by chance due to pressure or influence of any heavy party/powerful group/people then courts in that 120 years the case will be pending

(due to courts are setup as sikandare azam's time) manual, type-writers, retarded environment, bribing every person asking 10-20-500-5000 rupees and in 120 years you will be waiting for queue that your turn will come leave the remedy or solution anything like that you will get through court

KPK POLICE STATIONS: In Paksitan PTI the fake & most corrupt ever group which is claiming revolutionizing Pakistan, bringing change in atmosphere in thana and decoration of thana, however online fir, online case in court (in pakhtoon khuah will not be possible also, Jackets of commandos and higher to bigger to smaller amount of weapon is sold in Quetta, and in majority of the areas of Baluchistan Police doesn't exist at all also

In Baluchistan:

Indian and Iranian proxy agents, criminals & Aghani gangs working for human trafficking and terrorist in Pakistan for blast and against government or civilians and terrorism in public India and Iran facilitates, and to facilitate Iranian and Indian agents our local people are ready to cooperate with them, pay them 500,000 or 1,000,000 or 5,000,000 rupees and they can blast anyone or can kill anyone (due to value of human life comes with education religious or technical) From Zulfiqar Ali Bhutto to Ziaul Haq to Altaf Husain Nawaz Shareef Benazir Zardari Imran khan "they can do speeches"

In Flood and Power:

Baglihar Dam
Baglihar Dam, also known as Baglihar Hydroelectric Power Project, is a run-of-the-river power project on the Chenab River in the southern Doda district of the Indian state of Jammu and Kashmir

Baglihar Dam - Wikipedia, the free encyclopedia
*https://en.wikipedia.org/wiki/**Baglihar_Dam***

Sarobi Dam - energypedia.info
*https://energypedia.info/wiki/**Sarobi_Dam***

Sep 3, 2012 - Country: Afghanistan. City/Town: *Sarobi* district, Kabul. Coordinates (Powerhouse): 34° 35' 11" N, 69° 46' 33" E. Year of Commission: 1957.

We are getting flood since 5 8 years, every year Due to Bagliaar and Sarobi Damn Indo-Afghan-Pakistan Border Jurisdiction we are getting flood every year, beaurucrates of Sindh they have land coming in side or in map of the "kala bagh damn" and other damns in Pakistan,

Makhdoom Ameen Faheem who was feudal and Zardari kicked him out and He lived his end time period as Political orphan, then till his death, His 3 sisters are married with holy quran, it doesn not mean "some non muslim ask the girl have to do sex with quran "nauzubillah", it means that female will never ever have sex, will never ever marry in her life, 3 sisters,

 Makhdoom Amin Faheem married with Holy Quran, No Mullah or Council of Islamic Ideaology or court of law or council of Islamic idealogy, their own party? Will take notice of it, due to they are living in Dubai, Zurich, they are hiding behind cameras, behind law enforcement agencies, to whom they are paying day and night, and they are making more law enforcement mafia rich, and making pathway for them to come in power in elections of 2016, 2017 or whenever it will be elections

"According to Khabrain, a large number of feudals in Sindh had married their daughters to the Quran. The ceremony took place after the girl of the family was asked to take a bath, after which a Quran was put before her as the men folk apologised to her for the ritual which would condemn the girl never to get married but to read the Quran every day. In Sindh, **MPA Shabbir Shah?s sister**, ex-minister Murad Shah?s sister and two daughters, **three daughters of Mir Awwal Shah of Matiari**, daughters and sisters of Sardar Dadan and Nur Khan of the Lund tribe, **nieces of Sardar Ghulam of Mahar tribe**, and **the daughters of the Pir of Bharchundi** Sharif, were all married to the Quran to prevent

their share of the land going to them and thus avoid
redistribution of land.[Uzma Mazhar] "

Image of Interview of Allama Iqbal (The Poet of East's Daughter in law Interview,
Published by newspaper) However in Pakistan, Media Discuss women's rights and
Divorce/Marriage/Consent/Islamic laws or Pakistan Penal code law
His son after his death, got a leading remarkable victory on his seat, and He is Peer/Spiritual Leader/Fake
Spiritual leader & typical feudal Politician, who are living & dying for power & money).

PTI CHIEF MINISTER was crying in 1 speech, we are spending that much from budget, no project finance from overseas companies in form of usd/euro we can get, due to we are blind by birth, we never find the project finance companies

1. Who can setup Aviation Factories to Every sector they can develop

   2.construction, agriculture, land development, courts, police, homeless people, subsidiary in fuel/food, subsidiary in Ramadan or Project Finance for Desalination of sea, schooling, higher schools, universities, health centre we are blind by birth

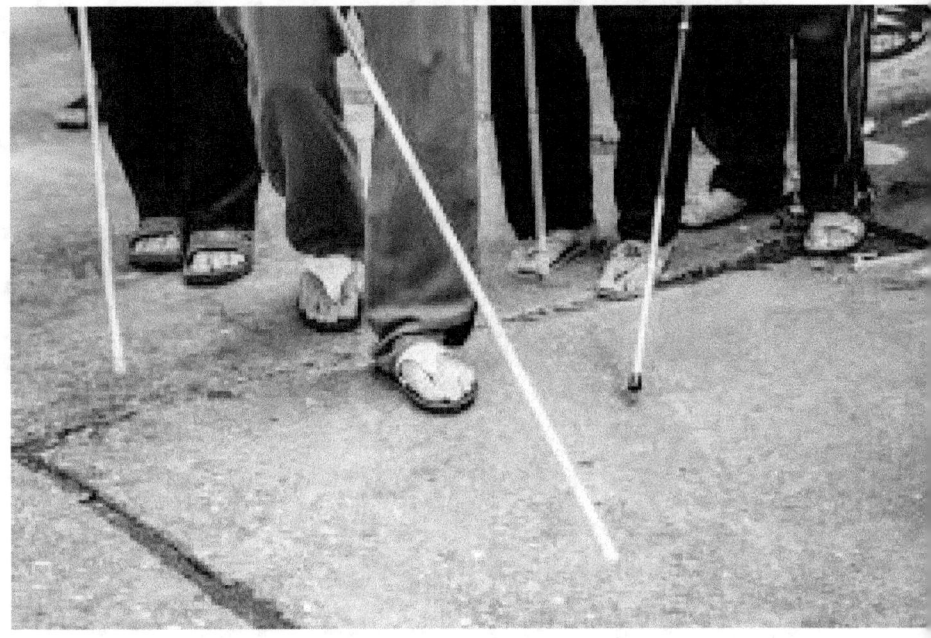

   3.we have considered that it will be done by "arbaabe ikhtiaar" a person who don't have any ikhtiaar or not a

nazim/counselor can do that also must have international affairs

4. Coal to Hydel to Wind to any project which can produce that much electricity which would be sufficient for us, in 120 years Inshallah we will not do that, right now at this time of writing this "watching news on Pakistani news channel "dunya tv" females are saying "people are dying in heat & Ramadan and during fasting, announced and non announced 8-12 hrs or

After 1 hr alternative electricity they are giving, bills are sending 25% more" Dunya News's News Caster saying that "announced and non announced Load Shedding is continued in Lahore"

SINDH COAL, BEAURUCRACY & HUR-RUHANI PAISHWAA MAFIA:

They are paishwaa of Huroon key ruhani paishwaa "Paghara Group Mafia" then Talpure Mafia, then Zardari Mafia, Then Bhutto Mafia they will never allow anyone to get educated primary schools in 68 years, dead and destroyed conditions the girls or females specially if they are educated then it will be issue, females will ask them questions or raise some issues socially or politically

So they need like cow/buffalo and 2 3 marriages they do to produce 8-10 child in Pakistan

ZINA & ALCOHOL MAFIA:

Alcohol is banned item in Pakistan, SRO'S LAWS are made and clearing rulings are made in that much accuracy that non Muslim is allowed to get import or anything like that or banned item is cleared under high amount of bribing money paid for clearance,

Big parties annual per year/per annum amount in advance under bribing category, so no cargo of them would be stopped or counter threat from any other law enforcement agency they can get

2,000,0000.00PKR rupees is profit in Black & Red Label Whisky/Beer per container and 10 containers to 100 containers 2-3 agents can take from you, besides murree beuree & in Baluchistan smuggling of cargo and legally it is sold also undeclared legal but it is legal

Prostitution Mafia:

It is Ramadan highest rates of prostitution and prostitutes market in Pakistan in Ramadan this is, and prostitution have markets like very low to middle and very high category also, some of them are dancing in international dance parties also

Some of them are hired for Prime Minister Houses, President Houses, Bears & Whisky got arrested in Pakistan from parliament, Nabeel Gabol said live in television news channels that this is habit in Pakistan that Mujra/dance and sex and prostitutes are hired per night/day basis in Parliament lodges

Like Dubai, Hongkong, Bangkok we have prostitutes declared it is open and not hidden but in Pakistan it is very clear

SAAS BAHU, MARRIAGE, SEX SOAP DRAMA MAFIA:

Pakistani Youth is not able to do sex after they are adult

You can have sex with 100 females or 100 males in 5 years 2 years, but marriage is that much equivalent to dooms day judgment due to Indian and Marriage Mafia

Every Morning and News show shows that, telecast that

1.marriage is very special day, you have to wear that, you have to look like that, then comes beauty parlor mafia, then comes bridal dress mafia, then comes the morning show and Indian Pakistan (COLORS, SONY, URDU1, HUMTV, GEO KAHANI, STARPLUS) mafia in that no issue in this world is issue

Except marriage and "Pakistan is Hindu" traditionalist society since generations

According to my Friend I was speaking to him on skype in UAE, He Said Dr sahib Pakistani male will come here, will have 20-50 girl friends, how much he can handle, after 5-8 years, he will go to his country, by saying that my mother decided my marriage with my cousin with phupi ki beti o with anyone other in relative

And UAE/ARAB COUNTRY RAISED man is the man which will be the person in 2nd meeting or 1st she will ask woman/girl that you are married and if yes is the answer, he will avoid/cut off with that woman/girl even He will not stop his car near to her anywhere also, and if answer is NO, He will ask to get married in 2nd or 3rd meeting he will get married in afternoon/evening time period with flowers & dry fruits people come and greet them

HAYAKALLAH/BARAKALLAH/MARBOOR Congratulations on wedding

Everyone is not sheikh/billionaire/rich in uae but lower middle class are not affected by HINDU STARPLUS HINDI BANGLA DRAMA affected since generations we are not muslims we are HINDU TRADITION FOLLOWER IN RELATIONSHIPS

According to me after getting adult 1 of the most Noble and Serious and Mature thing you decide with your consent and you deal with them life time, good or bad or worst it is your relationships either business, personal or social what it is

We are Hindu follower at our own traditions due to MOTI BHAINS/BUFFALOW type Khawateen and Marriage trend makers and Marriage and "shaaadi ho rahee hey" you don't know this is rasam and a person who is not married definitely how would he know that it is rasam or not?

Morning shows, suits, dresses, makeup, herbalist or tokey/manjan are everything is sponsor their advertisement they are paid and nothing is free, due to they are earning money through viewership of it

We are PURE HINDU IN RELATIONS TRADITIONS, NO CONEPTOF MARRIAGE WITHOUT GOLD AND DOWRY, In Hinduism there is no concept of

Inheritance for woman, they worship woman, they kill woman, female child, Highest rate of Female Infanticide in any country is in India?

World Biggest Aids Colony is in India 40% Aids Population of the world is living in India out of 100 Aids patient 40 are there in India, India is Tawaifzaad/Prostitute promoter society in the world, Maximum Number of females are Kindnapped and used and marketed and trafficked for prostitution and life time destiny for females is prostitution and to be used and utilized by them

India is the country in which Female's population is more than male, otherwise throughout the world females are 1 is to 3 1 is to 5 in numbers throughout the world, except Africa and India

In Africa people are dying with AIDS AND MALNUTRITION AND IN INDIA due to highest rate of female infanticide/abortion

MUHAJIR MAFIA:

Altaf Hussain killer of millions of females & males, children sitting in London in protocol of Queen Elizbeth with Kings are coming step by step Tony Blair to David Cameroon but He will remain King of Killers, when PMLN & Chaudhry Nisar are there, till that time they are settle due to Rights given to Rangers in Karachi Pakistan, due to Zardari, Faryal Talpure, Tapi, Qaim Ali Shah Whole Sindh Government are financier and Pure Financier of Terrorism mafia they import terrorist also

Then after it confessions of Uzair Baloch came in the end that launches/boats filled with $ they sent to uae, and money laundering network in dubai/zurich NO FIA,CIA or anyone will caught, due to they are with every terrorist & corrupt person in Pakistan, what are the cases on courts, in media it comes, they are innocent or civilian criminals

But beaurucarcy and gang ruling mafia no person of them will be caught in 200 years, this is guaranteed

In Pakistan Altaf Hussain created the lie we speak urdu, "Muhajir's Language" how it can be urdu, it can be hindi due to Raaj Bhasha of India is Hindi, after it Gujraati, Marathee, Malyalam, Wailam, Kashmiri, Bhojpuri, Telgu or anything like that but urdu is their language? How in top 17 languages In India no one speak this language, after 20 Lakhnawee & Ali Garh's Urdu Acsent is common in India

Cartoon Published in Newspaper about mandate of Altaf Hussain

Altaf Hussain collected 1,500,0000.00PKR PER DAY from Karachi Pakistan, stopped now due to Chauhdry Nisar and Rights given to Rangers so LIYARI GANG WAR+ANP+SUNNI TEHREEK ARE RESTING, Rangers are destined to arrest them, they cannot punish them through their courts,

Cartoon 2, Published in News Paper 2

Due to they have to handover them to courts, in courts pay the money, 99% criminals are resting at home, taking day and night chicken soup and tea, Breakfast, Lunch, Dinner VIP, Waiting for that time period when Bilawal or Zardari will come in power and

Inshallah then aseefa and bakhtawar will come on streets to distribute foods to due to Bilawal, Bakhtawar & Aseefa don't have any career in the world, no where they can earn 1billion pkr in 3 months, it will come with 1,000,000 weapon to be imported via sea customs, iran/Baluchistan border,

Through India & Iran then Inshallah 100 Pakistan Army soldiers and Iranian or Indian Soldiers will be killed and then they will be coming on channels or commenting on tweets "so sad that afghanis/indians on borders" they are doing it on border" people will mark it statement of Head of State Ruling Mafia's Son's Statement (this is our destiny what we are written for)

Images of Home & Altaf Hussain Holding British Passport

RELIGIOUS MAFIA:

Jamate Islami (the terrorist based college wings party like mqm, iso, and other militant terrorist organization In pakistan, Altaf Hussain hate islam due to He Hate Jamate Islami, Peoples party hates Islam due to they hate General Ziaul Haq)

Molana Fazlur Rehman a political career worshipper, smuggler, drugs, weapon, afghani, local and foreign terrorist supporter, says that He works for Islamic system, however his destiny remain to worship leaders, mafias, gangs in his whole life time

Jamate Islami, country is Islamic, Nation is Islamic, People are Muslims, in 68 Years they don't came in power, due to people collectively hate them, they are terrorist based mafia working on the name of international jihad, never went for any jihad, sent others only and let other die, we will die on our homes

Jamate Islami's people they are 1 eye blind and more than abul ala modudi they never find any scholar or anything and in any political gang based practice, the Islamic local terrorist group, who cares about local politics, and welfare and charity organization they were, in 1947-1957 they were revolutionary party, after 1957, they became Islamic party, which is party of Islamic type system and inside system change demanding party

And today result is mafia, gangs, terrorist, inflation, corruption, robbery, murder, extortion everything is on top, but what is happening, Sirajul haq is travelling in train march, non sense, Imran khan will come on streets, everyone is digging his own or her own hole, and waiting let the water/severage water will come

No party/group is sincere with Pakistan, anything they don't want to invest in Pakistan, infect Imran khan's and zardari's son remain outside Pakistan 12 months, and due to Imran khan is divorced and his sons few time came in jalsas, but Bilawal and bakhtwar and aseefa came few times, due to they know that billions of dollars per year they can get, is only due to 5000 neck if they will cut in liyari, their father and father's sister faryal talpure then billions of dollars money they can earn only in this case

In uk/uae/zurich they can sent billions of dollars, via launches/boats via smuggling through uzair baloch, so waiting for the next turn of them

MEDIA AND DESTINY OF PAKISTAN:

100 of the anchors are speaking in Pakistan on TV Channels, some are giving directions about laws, examples of Saudi, Malaysian, Arab, Western Countries, what to do, wait for next jalsa, wait for next election, then wait for new "faces/hands" will be changed and mafia will rule the land, mafia will rule the image of Pakistan

Bilawal, Bakhtawar, Aseefa, they don't have any job/employment business in the rest of the world, they know themselves that Rehman Malik, Dr Babar Awan, Asif Zardari Murdered Benazir Bhutto and Benazir Bhutto & Zardari combinely murdered Meer Murtaza Bhutto, they know it

Image of Aseefa, Bakhtawar, Bilawal, Sherry and other pppp members, still they are selling this grave/slogans of their mother/grandfather, however their name & slogans can give nothing to Pakistan in 2016 and onwards time period

But they come to Pakistan, they have millions of acres property Bilawal houses in Karachi, Lahore, Behria town, millions of money for bribing in manual work, registration, legal all of the drafting, political work in Sindh, in institution they are mafia, their own people are employed, and 1 thing they have done MQM, PPPP and every Sindh mafia everyone has to document and submit documents according to "pre-requisites" then pay them the amount then you will be on board on job

TANKER, TRANSPORT, WATER HYDRANTS MAFIA:

Image of hydrant mafia, workers, to every permission/jurisdiction/moment/filling/timing everything they are paid for that, millions of people don't have water, their life time destiny is to move from this country/die in this state and pay for this water

Image, The most sophisticated transport where passengers are travelling with safety and security same as Bilawal, Imran khan, Zardari, Nawaz Shareef, Aseefa, Bakhtawar can never dream at Night

Your life is in hand of God, Do the suicide man, No Transport for you, God destined this miraculous transport for you, Heavenly Routed, Direct to Hell/Heaven (Deeds you have your own, when you die)

Pathaan remain the owner of hydrant and water mafia, mqm hold the water board mafia like leech and parasite since last 10-20 years, if you are living in Karachi, you will find people who are employeed in water board, they are employeed on 35,000 25,000 per month salary, in 6 months, they never visited water board,

But 15,000 they got every month, and some people inside water board they mark their attendance and per month salary in documents and records sent to every employee as budget of water board and in audit it is submitted and never ever auditor will say anything also, due to they also need money and they are in Pakistan also,

(Life at 0% risk, die your own death, its destiny, its Government of Zardari, Nawaz, General Ziaul Haq or
Musharraf we are born as Animals, and we will live and die like Animals, God willingly Inshallah, this is our written destiny)

So they know this is green land and green land can provide unlimited black money definitely everyone is criminal here, so you have a lot of scope in auditing also to earn money

Election in 2016, 2017, 2018:

Only faces will be changed, new people will come they will do 10-20% changes, and will say that we will do that, we will do that, armed forces, law enforcement agencies knows that who are political and criminal mafia, they charge money from them and educated man will take "overseas skilled immigration" or "work permit" and will go abroad and no destiny of them as educated and intellect people we have in Pakistan

IMRAN KHAN'S MOST CORRUPT PARTY Inside Mafia and Outside supporting mafia, will be waiting for alliance with Asif Ali Zardari to come in Power

Imran Khan will be joining Mqm's Half wing in Sindh, due to in Sindh with Jamate Islami and PMLN association they are defeated in worst manner, then establishment made MQM IN 2 parts, MQM (MUSTAFA KAMAAL), MQM ALTAF HUSSAIN, MQM AFAQ AHMED MUHAJIR(WHICH is approximately a dead chapter wing of mqm)

WHAT USA/G20/ISLAMIC COUNTRIES, INTERNATIONAL COUNTRIES WILL RECOMMEND US:

That it is internal issue of Pakistan
Election commission, manual, online, balloting result if you need in your favor then pay 20-80crore PKR for 1 night, then get results, and rest of the result the process, litigation in system, endorsed by mafia is equivalent to the time period, voting, balloting, counting, re-checking, verification in next 10 years,

You will not get any result, till the time period 2 times tenure government Imran khan will be completing and shedding dirt/blood and alleged charges of corruption with his emotional speeches and result will be big zero for Pakistan and Pakistani Politics

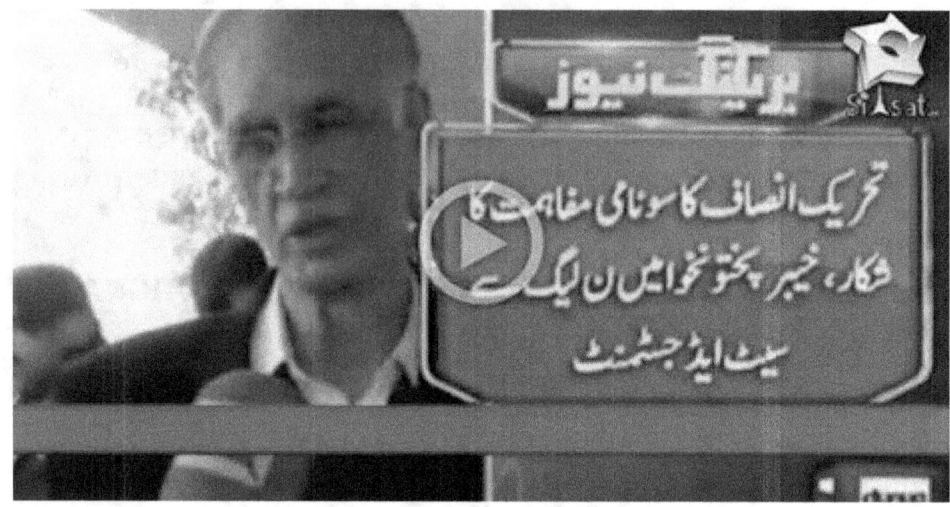

Imran khan delivered 100's of the speeches,

1. They will build the computerized system, e-system, bio-metric system to cast, check, verify, re-verify the vote, verified with cnic, family number, voting number, voting turn, token number (no software, device, systematic software for that is introduced, due to we know that with this system, probably we can get 100 votes, and system introduced, but in politics you need massive/rigging how much you can do, then you can come in power yourself (this is system of Pakistan)

2.Molvi/Religious people will tell you

1.we are disobedient to Allah, We don't follow shariah, Islamic commandments, we are lier, cheater, fraud, and every un-human habit & skills we have, due to that is wrath of Allah/God Almighty and this type of people are ruler on us, they are insulting abusing our old people & childrens?

But these people & mafia will be governing and ruling party in Pakistan, either in form of Bani Gala & Lal Haweli Mafia or Tahirul Qadri or Religious or Secular Mafia or 100-150 families mafia? Beaurucracy and law enforcement mafia?

2. Ethical commanding people, Journalist will tell us, we have to educate our nation, 70-90% population don't have religious/technical education, for which we need adult and primary, higher, secondary and higher secondary, university, Islamic & technical education,

   But journalist will tell us we have to educate our nation, by watching HBO, CARTOON NETWORK, HUMTV, STARPLUS, the nation is going to get educated after watching breaking news that child is died by falling in man-hole in Federal B AREA KARACHI, LAHORE RAILWAY STATION YARD IN Pakistan

3. Some people will tell you that we don't have exact curriculum of country, primary, higher, secondary education we have to change it, and Journalist will tell you, G20 countries will dictate us, that this is internal issue, with Taliban, nato forces, space air/ground required or what is required, they will cooperate, they will do it with the help of mafia, they will negotiate and they will handle with mafia

4. The Journalist, Media, Taliban, Religious, Secular Mafia will keep on guiding/suggesting us, nothing will happen in Pakistan, In Pakistan list of 100-500-2000-5000 top level People,

   Until and unless you will not shed the blood of these people, Mafia will be ruling party (as religious & secular mafia) in Pakistan, and no change will come in Pakistan in any institute/departments/courts/system on federal, provincial and metropolitan level.

What forced me to write this:
1.we don't have education, primary, higher, secondary, university, research level no project, foreign investment,

projects, education loan, problems, affairs of education, drafting laws for education, male & female (adult & minors)

no one in Pakistan will come to build that, due to all of the people can deliver emotional speeches, they are living like kings, Imran khan A single un-married person lives in 7000sq yard home, some are living in Bilawal house,

Some are living in lal haweli, some are in raiwind mehel, religious people justifies it that it is allowed in shariah also, if money is not earned through corruption, I say to them, then don't give call for social and justice based revolution, you are not from the background of people,

You don't understand what is issue, you can come on stage, can deliver emotional speeches, press conferences, can criticize each other, insult each other, that's what so far they have done in Pakistan, they will do in future also

2. We have daily political talk shows, anchors who are known as intellect people who are discussing international afghani, irani, india and british,American,

war, social, Islamic, political issues, infect this is wastage of time & money, we don't need that much gibrish or programs candidate for each party have price, in which talk show, how much money for seat you have to pay, which candidate of which party will come in program against which person of which party is "pre-decided"

3. A news anchor, media all of them are only and only earning money through hiding their blackmailing, then comes urdu print media then they praise the leaders, political situation by using references of Islamic shariah, history and political social commandments, laws, reference "to the nation, in which 70-80%" people are illiterate and they don't have any religious/technical education

4. Religiously people are emotionally used, and these channels earn money in Ramadan gift schemes, jackpot schemes, and in sectarian religious propagation, media & media houses knows that

   1. There is no government/system of religious research based education

   2. There is no institution in Pakistan, who is teaching people the religious/technical education from primary, secondary, university, higher level of education so they use this for the earning

   3. In Rabiul awal they will propagate 12th Rabiul awal Eid, which is fabrication/bidah/innovation in Islam

   4. On 10th of Muhrram they will celebrate the matam/noha 1st to 10th Ramadan all channels are paid to play the clips of matam/noha/jalsey/juloos & shame ghareebaan

   5. Whole year, 11 months, they insult, abuse, criticize,

hard hit tingly criticize mullah and on the 12th month, they will use them for earning money to do sehar and aftaar transmissions

Nawaz Shareef, Zardari, Molana Fazlur Rehman, Asfand Yar Wali, Sheikh Rasheed they are born to rule us, they are born as ruler, their progeny's slavery is our destiny, due to they are born as rulers, we are born to vote for them, a technical/religious non educated blind nation's citizen

The Pakistani, This is my destiny, not destined by Allah or Muhammad Saw but the democratic, constitution, law enforcement, beaurucary, gang mafia they decided it, and I am forced to follow them, due to I am born as slave, my father, my fore-fathers died "in struggle for self existence" in earning money for day night wife, sons/daughters and pro-creation

What Pakistan means, we get aid/donations/begging money from IMF, KSA AID, in order to defend our position that we are WITH USA, KSA and in future Afghanis, Indians, Iranis or In War, what is going to be happened, We are behind 500 years, from the world, from uae/usa/uk/eu countries

We will remain 500 years behind, due to
1.Bhutto is alive here in Pakistan
2.Gangs & Mafia are ruling parties always and democracy is in danger
3.Molvi Mafia & Secular Gangs are Ruling Party and Islam is in danger
it will remain in danger for next 168 Years

Allah is witness over it, Human History is witness over it Without Massive Bloodshed there is no revolution came in any country, any nation without massive bloodshed

Every Armed forces or Democratic Leader came had complexion of inferiority complex, he/she want to live in palaces, want to spend billions of dollars, want security and protocols and want and want to spend 22million for fixing of wash room of prime minster, want to eat dinner in which 50

cuisines are waiting on table, which 45 you don't even touch/taste (we are inferior and born with inferiority complex, prostitution, sex, unlimited money, we are not able to move from this mentality)

2nd Biggest Mentality we are not able to move from this mentality also, that is Business tycoon, mafia, 100-1000's people bowing you/prostrating you that you have that much money, In Pakistan Nihari Hotel, to Sweets, Cattle House, Slaughter House,

Stock Exchange Brokerage, Karachi/Pakistan stock listed companies, investment, securities mafia they use/spent their money to show the people on every event, Ramadan, eid or any event, that we have that much money

However for public transport to power to any project, if they can build in Pakistan, will not, due to in that they will not get any publicity/advertisement of their name Behria town/Malik Riaz can build the biggest mosque, University on the name of Mafia/gangster/murder/target killer's gang's leader in Karachi Altaf Hussain but no public transport in Pakistan, for setup of whole cost, what it will be in 5billion$ or 10 billion$ we will not do that

HOSPITAL/MEDICAL/PHARMACEUTICAL MAFIA:

In Pakistan we don't have instrument for Zika virus test, medical counsellation or any institute are not able to convince people that they are not mixing any solution/drug that will make them infertile, forever, permanently disable to produce any child in further therefore 100's of deaths of females and males came in existence, but due to a lay man don't trust physician

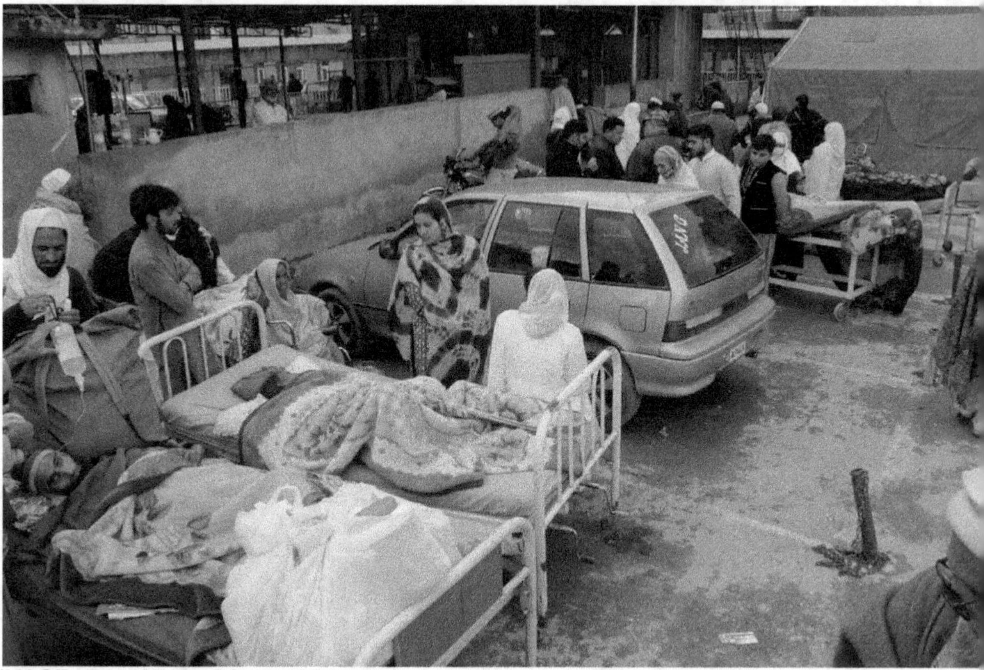

IMAGE (PAKISTANI GOVT HOSPITALS)

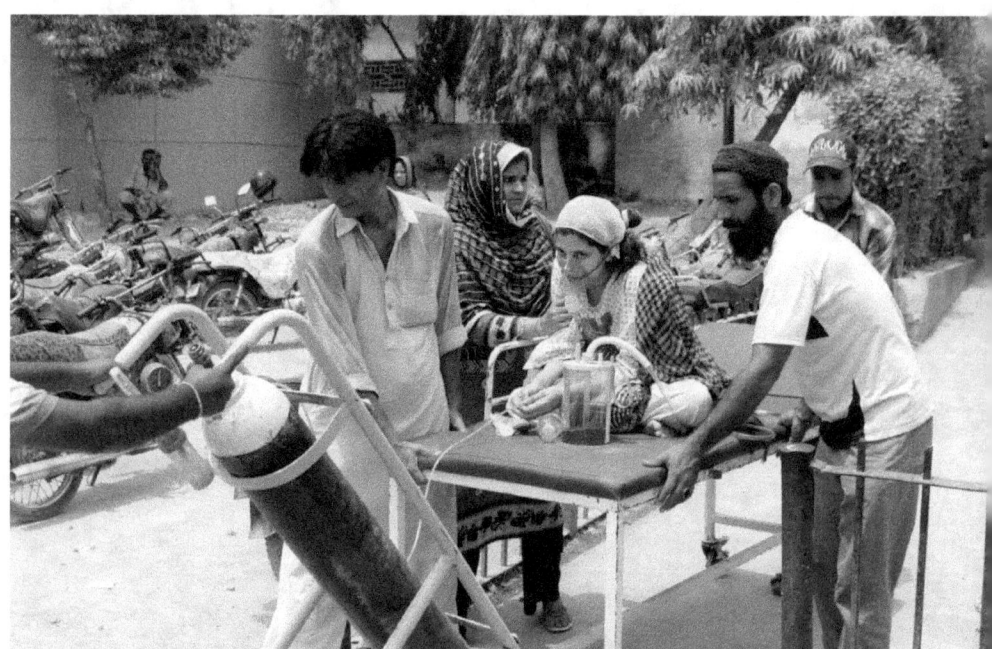

IMAGE (PAKISTANI GOVT HOSPITALS)

IMAGE (PAKISTANI GOVT HOSPITALS)

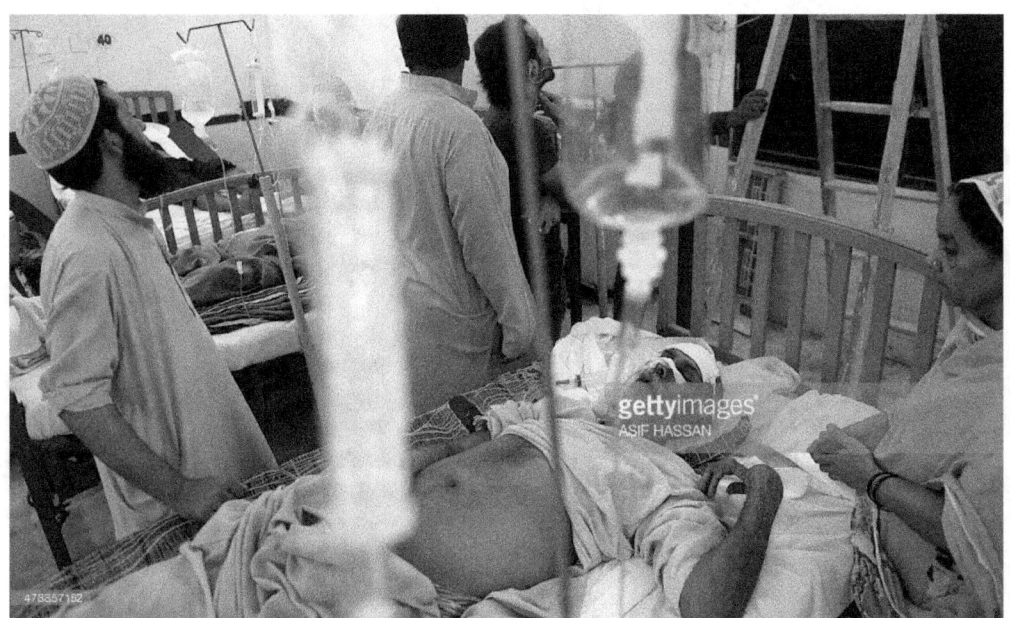

IMAGE (PAKISTANI GOVT HOSPITALS)

We have no board of alternative medicine, homeophathic, alternative medicines no board or certified practitioner license, research laboratories, research institutes, who have pathological and clinical pathological, bio-chemisty labs,

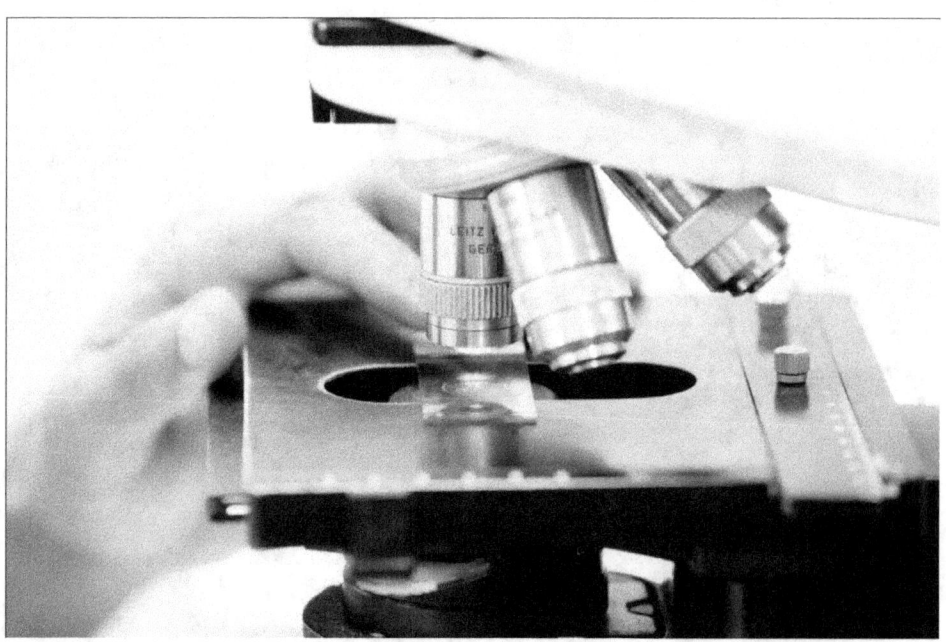

BIOCHEMISTRY

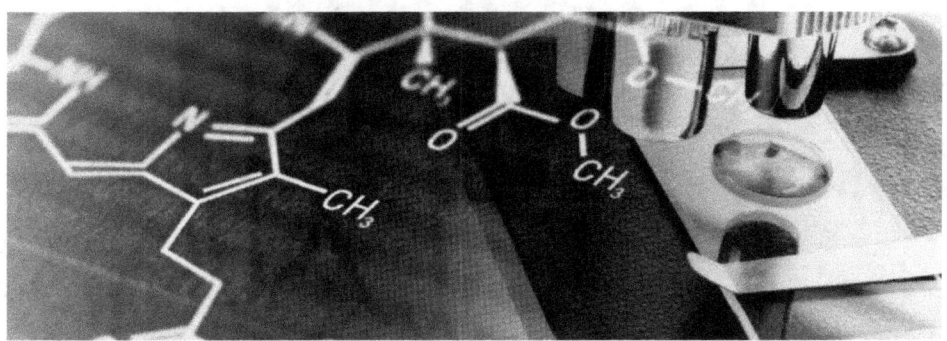

In which new medications they can invest/discover/test like Chineese medicines, they sold over medicine equivalent to 1,000,000$ in 1 year, before 3 years, the flower, stems, roots and medicines not only they are cultivating and exporting throughout the world in category of herbal medicine export

Due to our destiny is eastern medicine, Chineese medicines multi level marketing medicines and no certified, degree, diploma, research, institutes, universities we have on state level who can issue professional degree

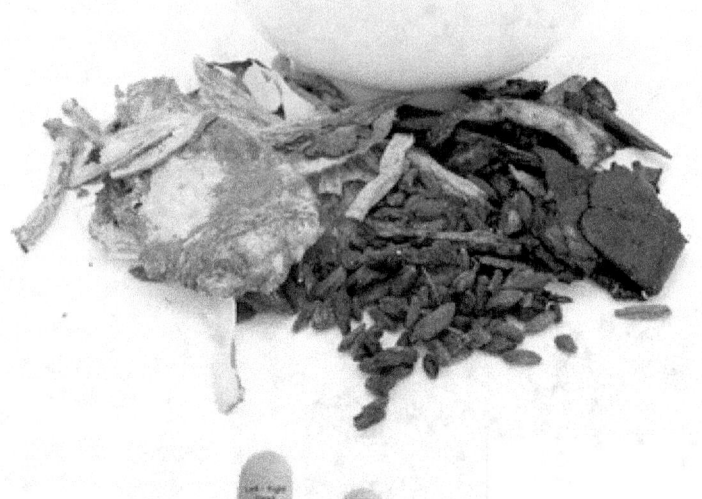

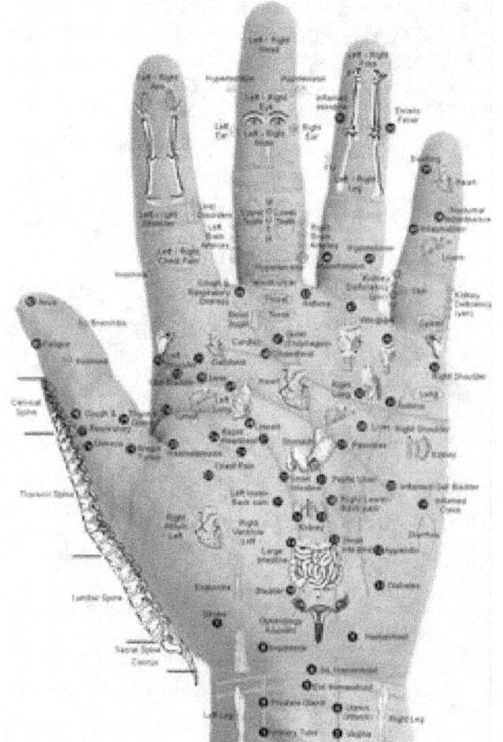

In Pakistan veterinarian and zoologist and agriculture experts we can produce, we have land which can be used for cultivation of jatropha, rapeseed oil (it is seed like mustard) and seeds, oil of that mixing with alcohol and caustic soda we can make biodiesel can export upto 1,000,000 mton a month in eu countries and countries who are going for alternative energy projects, a project finance company and investments and lendings non interest based as Oman, Malaysia are doing it under Islamic finance, Swift society is also investing in Islamic Finance

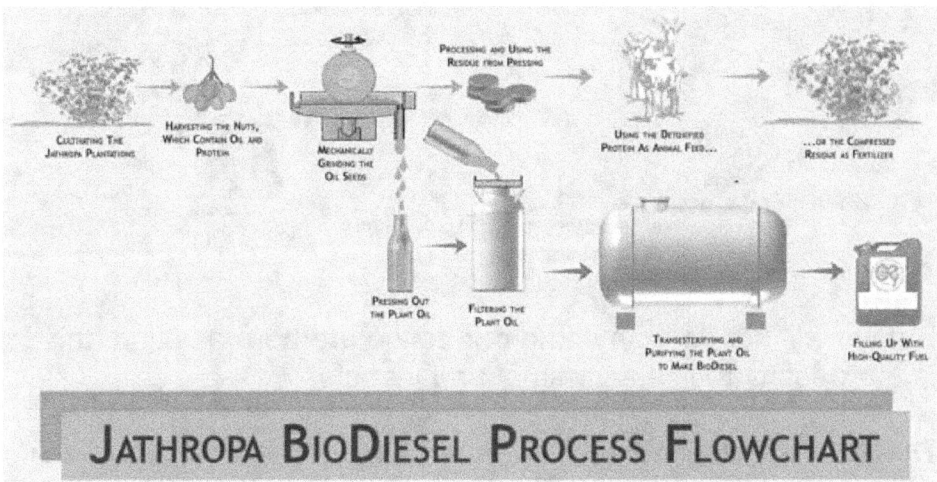

JATHROPA BIODIESEL PROCESS FLOWCHART

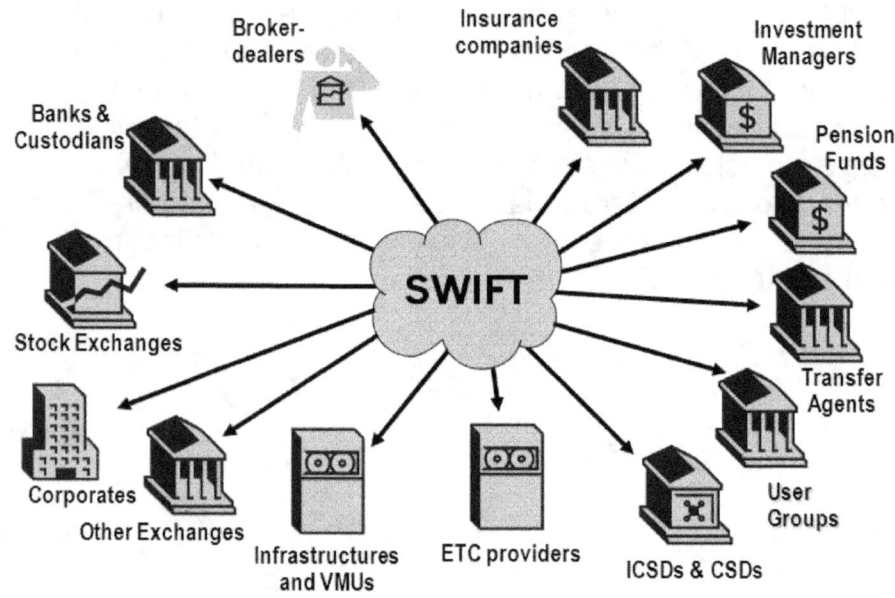

But we will not do it anything due to we are born as blind, this is our destiny to live as animal and insects

Due to for zoologist, faculties, environment, distance learning or elearning any course, without space, university, online, e-education we can introduce, but we will not do private examinations (admissions open for 100,000 or 1,000,000 students) without fees Pakistani government is not able to do, what they can do before 20 years it was marks of Hafize Quran and Highest percentage candidate will get Admission in Medical & Engineering College,

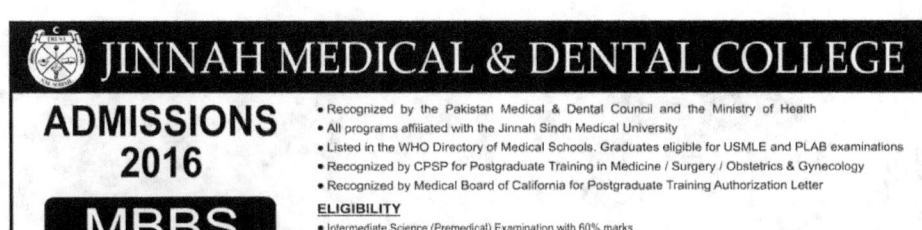
It is well known fact that genius person don't need counseling and advice and they can do studies in usa/uk/eu countries, Australia and any other countries and the one who is failure, not genius, or average/below average student like Srilanka 100% literacy rate countries we can produce, but we will not do, we will not do

Due to We have Genius like Dr Asim who is owner of hospitals, in board of medical counsellation will be facilitating target killer and mqm & liyari peoples party terrorists and and after it Inshalalh no FIA,CIA and other will arrest any persons, 100-1000's the judges will not hand them also, due to everyone is paid too much paid, no one will dare in 100 years to do any decision which will single him in this system, due to everyone is nude in this system and everyone want to remain nude in this sytem

Pharmaceutical Industries and Dr's and Health Centre Mafia:

1. No one will write the drug name, they will write brand name, due to 600 plus pharmaceuticals, they are exporting it, in black they are selling it, expired medicines they are also selling it in villages, people are dying it due to it Alhamdulillah also,

   And every year 1 consignment, they track, arrest and destroy and 99% they sell in Hospitals, Clinics, Dispensaries, now if you will question, health inspector or anyone, who want to do some action who don't want to do, it's your will and 80% and above people believe in earning money,

   So pharmaceutical, MRI, XRAY, Laboratory and for everything marketing and selling it is 1st priority of everyone in Pakistan and majority of the people are technically, medically and religiously un-educated and this is our destiny to get black-mailed by every industry, every department, every health centre, every medical practitioner also

3.In Pakistan in Hyderabad Isra Medical college have 845,000/- per annum fees for MBBS and 465,000/- for self finance/overseas seats is the fees, 12-130,0000.00PKR x 5 =850,0000.00PKR is the cost in which anyone will do the MBBS, why he will consider any factor about humanity or anything, preach him/her religion or anything (He will be part of medical counsellation and drug, health centre mafia)

4.The one who can afford, will be their client, and you will become then the respected and honorable client of them and they will be respected reputable doctors "so with 1 eye, 1 ear hearing capability, able to understand some people will be destiny of these physicians

I AM PAKISTANI, I BORN AS SLAVE SON OF SLAVE/SLAVE/SLAVE

WILL REMAIN SLAVE/SLAVE/SLAVE OF THESE 100-150 FAMILIES IN PAKISTAN

یہ ایک نظریاتی غلط فہمی ہے کہ پاکستان اسلام کی خاطر بنا

یہ بنا 100-150 خاندانوں، بدماشوں، سرداروں، عیاش فحاش لوگوں کے لئے

ہم تو پیدا ہوئے ہیں ان کی لونڈی اور رعایا کے طور پر اور ہماری حیثیت رینگتے ہوئے کیڑوں کی ماند ہے اس زمین پر، جن کا مقدر جوتوں سے کُچلا جانا ہے آج یا کل۔

IT IS MISCONCEPTION THAT PAKISTAN CAME INTO EXISTENCE ON THE NAME OF ISLAM, IT CAME INTO EXISTENCE FOR 100-150 FAMILIES,
Traitors, Criminals, Gangs, Hooligans, Sardaars, Feudals, who love prostitution and drinking and we are born as slave of them, our destiny is sex slave of them, and like warms crawling on earth, today/tomorrow to come under their feets today/tomorrow is our destiny

I as Pakistani accept and admit that

The Pakistani, This is my destiny, not destined by Allah or Muhammad Saw but the democratic, constitution, law enforcement, beaurucary, gang mafia they decided it, and I am forced to follow them, due to I am born as slave, my father, my fore-fathers died "in struggle for self existence" in earning money for day night wife, sons/daughters and pro-creation

Mafia is ruling the system, since the time we got freedom from India

Peace be on you, on your Progeny, On Your Family
Pakistan Zindabaad o Paindabaad, Wasalam Ismaiel
والسلام اسماعیل۔ (A Pakistani, Who is born as Pakistani, Will Die as Pakistani).

www.ingramcontent.com/pod-product-compliance
Lightning Source LLC
Chambersburg PA
CBHW071214280526
45787CB00002B/680